DISCOVER THE **MOST AMAZING** LOCOS ON EARTH

MEGA BOOK OF
TRAINS

INTERNET LINKED

CHRYSALIS CHILDREN'S BOOKS

INTERNET LINKS

http://www.steamlocomotive.com
Find out about railway museums, surviving steam locomotives, steam types and lots more.

http://howstuffworks.com
Learn how engines work – and more!

http://www.ukrail.uel.ac.uk
Here is a steam locomotive picture gallery, technical information, a locomotive database – and railways around the world.

http://www.scitoys.com
Find out how to make all kinds of science toys, including a simple steam engine.

http://www.railfan.net
Created by a real rail fan – for real fans! There are photos and information about all kinds of trains here.

http://www.trainnet.org
Here you'll find photos, recommended railway books and downloadable libraries.

http://www.imaginationstationkids.com
Click 'kids encyclopedia' for fun info about different locomotives.

http://www.tgv.com
Click 'English version' to read about the TGV, travel information and more.

http://www.railwaytechnology.com
For the latest technical info on high-speed, light and heavy railways.

http://www.monorails.com
This is the place to go for monorails.

http://www.o-keeting.com
Learn about some of the latest developments in high-speed rail across Europe and Japan.

INTERNET SAFETY

Always follow these guidelines for a fun and safe journey through cyberspace:

1. Ask your parents for permission before you go online.

2. Spend time with your parents online and show them your favourite sites.

3. Post your family's e-mail address, even if you have your own (only give your personal address to someone you trust).

4. Do not reply to e-mails if you feel they are strange or upsetting.

5. Do not use your real surname while you are online.

6. Never arrange to meet 'cyber friends' in person without your parents' permission.

7. Never give out your password.

8. Never give out your home address or telephone number.

9. Do not send scanned pictures of yourself unless your parents approve.

10. Leave a website straight away if you find something that is offensive or upsetting. Talk to your parents about it.

First published in the UK in 2002 by Chrysalis Children's Books PLC
The Chrysalis Building, Bramley Road, London, W10 6SP

Copyright © Chrysalis Children's Books
A ZIGZAG BOOK

Author: Lynne Gibbs
Editorial Director: Honor Head
Art Director: Sophie Wilkins
Senior Editor: Rasha Elsaeed
Designer: Scott Gibson
Picture Researcher: Terry Forshaw

Every effort has been made to ensure none of the recommended websites in this book is linked to inappropriate material. However, due to the ever-changing nature of the Internet, the publishers regret they cannot take responsibility for future content of these websites. Therefore, it is strongly advised that children and parents consider the safety guidelines above.

British Library Cataloguing in Publication Data for this book is available from the British Library.

ISBN 1 844580 22 9

Printed and bound in Taiwan

CONTENTS

Locomotives took off in the early 1800s. At this time, engines were powered by steam made from water heated by coal fires. On the following pages you can read about some of the greatest locomotives in history – from the first steam trains to hit the tracks, to the fastest and strangest in design and technology.

FORCE OF GRAVITY

The first railways were built in Europe over 250 years ago. They were used to carry coal from mines, loaded wagons or chaldrons. They could only run downhill on flat stone laid in the ground. Metal rails soon followed. The wheels had projecting rims (flanges) on either side to stop trucks from running off the tracks.

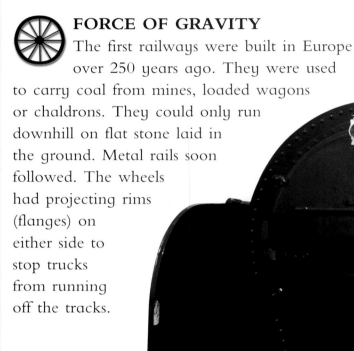

MEGA FACT

Built in 1960, Evening Star was the last steam locomotive built for British Rail. It was used for freight work and to pull passenger and express trains.

How a steam engine works

The diagram shows the inside of an 1840s locomotive. Burning coal in the fire box heats air in the boiler tubes, which boil water in the boiler. This creates steam, which collects in the dome. The driver can open a valve to let steam pass through the steam pipe and push pistons backwards and forwards. The pistons are connected by rods to the driving wheels and make them turn. The pistons also push exhaust steam up the blast pipe and out through the chimney. This draws the hot air from the fire box and helps the fire to burn well.

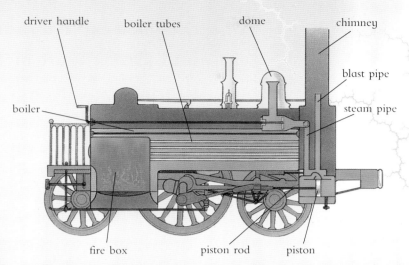

driver handle · boiler tubes · dome · chimney · blast pipe · steam pipe · boiler · fire box · piston rod · piston

> **MEGA FACT**
> *Until the early 1900s, horse-powered railways were used throughout the world to pull vehicles for passengers and freight.*

AT YOUR CONVENIENCE

Until 1882, passengers had to stay in one compartment until the train stopped, as there was no passageway for them to move from one compartment to another. In that year, cars with a side aisle came into service. At each end of the aisle was a restroom – one for ladies, the other strictly for gentlemen!

TRAINS TAKE TO THE TRACKS

Since the first practical steam engines were designed by Thomas Newcomen in 1712, and James Watt in 1769, engineers had tried to use steam power to drive a self-propelled vehicle. The first successful guided railway locomotives were designed and built in the early 1800s. In 1823, George and his son Robert Stephenson set up the world's first locomotive works in Newcastle-upon-Tyne, England. It built steam engines that were sold all over the world.

MEGA FACT
Until 1896, the speed limit for cars in Britain was just 3.2 km/h — that's the average person's walking pace!

ROCKET

Trevithick's steam locomotive

Richard Trevithick, from Cornwall, England, designed the first steam locomotive in 1804. It ran on rails for the South Wales Pen-y-Darren Iron Works. The locomotive was adapted from a stationary steam engine and was so heavy, that it shattered the tracks. This little 'mishap' delayed rail travel technology for another 20 years.

ROCKET RACES AWAY

In 1829, a group of British businessmen decided to build a railroad between Manchester and Liverpool. They could not decide whether to use horse-drawn carriages or cars pulled by a steam locomotive, so they announced a competition for anyone who could produce a reliable steam engine. Robert Stephenson built and entered the Rocket. The Rocket carried its own coal and water to make the steam that drove its wheels in a tender behind the driver. The loco achieved a world speed record of 58km/h, which was amazingly fast for its time.

MEGA FACT

In 1769, Frenchman Nicholas Cugnot built the first self-propelled vehicle in the world. But the three-wheeled steam-powered road vehicle was difficult to control and the project was abandoned.

STEPHENSON'S ROCKET

After the success of the Rocket, steam-powered locomotives developed rapidly and the railway industry expanded. The world's first railway trains steamed along in Britain, but soon many countries began to develop their own railway systems. As well as providing better and cheaper transport, rail travel created thousands of jobs.

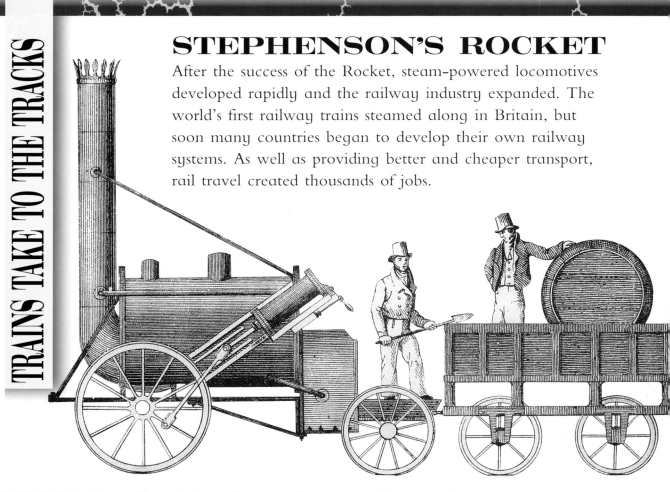

STIRLING 8ft SINGLE CLASS 4-2-2

Patrick Stirling, superintendent of England's Great Northern Railway, had the first Stirling Single built in 1870 at the line's own Doncaster Locomotive Plant. Its elegant lines, gleaming paint-work and polished brass trim make it one of the most beautiful engines ever made. The huge 2.4m-driving wheels allowed the engines to reach very high speeds. The engine had outside cylinders but inside valve chests – the slide valves being driven direct by sets of Stephenson's link motion. When the driver pulled the brake lever, a vacuum was created in the brake pipe. This pushed the brake shoes onto the wheels and stopped the train.

Best Friend of Charleston

The first full-size steam locomotive to be built in North America went into service on 15 January 1831. Constructed at the West Point Foundry in New York, Best Friend of Charleston ran on the South Carolina Railroad, North America's first commercial steam railway. Best Friend of Charleston travelled along the track at 32km/h. It handled a five-car train and carried over 50 passengers.

PUFFING BILLY

Puffing Billy was the first locomotive to operate commercially as a train using the idea of a smooth wheel on a smooth rail. It was built in 1813 by William Hedley to haul loaded coal wagons at about 7km/h from Wylam Colliery in Northumberland, England, to the River Tyne – a distance of 8km. The track was damaged by the locomotive's weight and had to be rebuilt. Because complaints were made about the noise and smoke that it made, Puffing Billy was modified so that the steam passed through a 'quieting' chamber before going up the chimney.

MEGA FACT
Because of the plentiful supply of coal, and to ease road traffic congestion, steam engines are still used in China today.

FLYING SCOTSMAN

In 1923, Flying Scotsman was the first express passenger locomotive to be built by the then newly formed London and North-Eastern Railway. Designed at cost of £7,944 (high in those days), it travelled at 633km/h. In 1934, Flying Scotsman was the first steam locomotive to achieve a speed of 160km/h. British Railways withdrew the world-famous locomotive from service in 1963. Over 70 similar locomotives were scrapped, leaving Flying Scotsman the sole survivor of its class. In 1977, the locomotive co-starred in the film *Agatha* with Dustin Hoffman. Then in 1966, it was sold for a staggering £1,250,000. A further £750.000 was spent rebuilding the classic to its former glory.

RM CLASS 4-6-2

China's RM Class 4-6-2 is thought to be the last steam express passenger locomotive in world. Construction of the RM (Ren Ming) class began in 1958 at the Szufang (Tsing-tao) Works. The main difference between the RM Class and almost all other steam engines outside the former Soviet Union states was the position of the main steam-pipe. This normally ran forward from the dome inside the boiler, but in these engines there was enough room for it to be placed in an insulated trunking above the boiler.

MEGA FACT
Isambard Kingdom Brunel (1806-1859) designed many of the great railways, bridges and tunnels in Britain.

Turbomotive 4-6-2

Turbine engines had been used for many years to power ships and electric generators, but they had not been widely used for locomotives. In 1932 William Stanier, Chief Mechanical Engineer of the London Midland & Scottish Railway, built a turbine locomotive to carry out an experiment. Turbine propulsion was carried out on a prototype 4-6-2.

The Turbomotive gave 500,000 kilometres of service. It looked promising, but there were problems. In 1951, following a failure of the main turbine, the express passenger locomotive was rebuilt into a normal 4-6-2 and named Princess Anne.

BIG BOY

Union Pacific's 500-tonne Big Boy is the world's largest, most powerful steam locomotive ever built. The engines were built in the 1940s to haul heavy freight trains uphill in Utah, USA. Before Big Boy, a helper service was needed. These locomotives could reach speeds of up to 130km/h, but produced a maximum continuous power of 113km/h. Twenty-five Big Boys were built. The first group, 'class 1', were built in 1941 and were numbered 4000-4019. The second group, 'class 2', were built in 1944 and were numbered 4020-4024. The last revenue freight pulled by a Big Boy was in July 1959.

MEGA FACT
In the 1840s, wealthy people travelled in their own covered carriages. The poor had to sit in open trucks. By 1850, railways provided covered carriages for all travellers.

DIESEL AND ELECTRIC LOCOS

The invention of diesel-powered and electric locomotives brought the age of steam to a close. Diesel-powered trains are often used on lines that are not busy, and where electrification of rails is uneconomical. The first electric trains were developed at the end of the 19th century. After World War II, many countries in Europe rebuilt their damaged railway systems by electrifying old lines as well as building new lines.

MEGA FACT

In the 1930s, diesel trains started to run in countries such as Germany and the USA, where diesel oil was cheaper than coal.

DIESEL VERSUS ELECTRIC

Electric locomotives are faster, quieter, easier to run than diesel, and do not emit smoke. There are more moving parts in a diesel engine than than in an electric engine, so friction is higher.

Inside a diesel-electric locomotive

Diesel oil burns with explosive force in cylinders in the engine. This drives pistons that in turn drive a generator, which makes electricity. The generator powers the traction motors that turn the locomotive's wheels. Extra electricity is stored in batteries. The radiator keeps the diesel engine cool, and the exhaust lets out used gases. Diesel engines are more efficient and smoother than steam locos, so do less damage to the railway track.

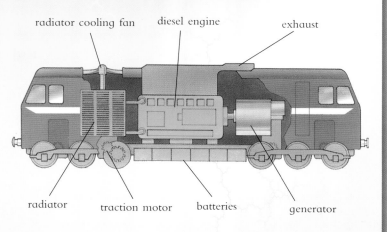

radiator cooling fan   diesel engine   exhaust

radiator   traction motor   batteries   generator

BIG, BOLD AND BEAUTIFUL

In 1969 the Union Pacific Railroad, known for its large steam locos, purchased the largest and most powerful diesel engine ever built – the DDA40X. Named Centennial, these 270-tonne, 29m-long beasts were powered by two engines providing 6600hp. In all, 47 units numbered 6900-6946 were purchased. Centennials were designed for high-speed freight and by 1980 had averaged 3 million kilometres a piece. Like the Big Boys, 113km/h was attainable with heavy tonnage trains on level track.

INTERCITY 125

The Intercity 125 diesel-electric high-speed train is common along main lines in the UK. An Intercity 125 is made up of two 'class 43' power cars, one at each end, and seven or eight passenger trailers in the middle. Being diesel engines, they are not particularly powerful, generating only 2250hp. This is why two of them are needed for high speeds. Australian rail based their high-speed XPT on the 'class 43' power cars, although the XPT is not as fast as its British counterpart.

Flying Hamburger

With its striking mauve and cream gleaming livery, the German-built Fliegender Hamburger (Flying Hamburger) set off on its first journey from Berlin to Hamburg on 15 May 1933, travelling at 124.5km/h. The Flying Hamburger was a two-car, articulated diesel unit with a 410hp engine mounted on each end bogie. There was accommodation for 98 second-class passengers in the two coaches and four seats at the small buffet.

Eurotram

Tramways were built throughout in Europe after the Second World War. Many of the lines have now disappeared, yet trams remain one of the most efficient ways of moving people efficiently, especially in heavily populated cities. In 1994 the Eurotram, built by ABB Transportation, came into service in Strasbourg, France. Operating on an entirely new system, it runs on reserved track, in-tunnel or in streets, and has a maximum speed of 21km/h.

CENTENNIAL

Centennials were designed to operate over all the Union Pacific main lines in the USA, unlike Big Boys. Both designs were unique to the Union Pacific, but they incorporated many of the best features of other up-to-date American locomotives. With the decline of freight transport, Centennials were taken out of circulation in 1980. During the economic recovery of 1984, 25 Centennials were then returned to service. But due to their high maintenance costs, most of these well-loved locomotives were retired again by 1986.

MEGA FACT
There are over 17,702km of track on the British railway system.

MEGA FACT
The electric tramway in Blackpool, England, is only one of three systems in the world to use double-deck cars.

15

DELTIC

Otherwise known as the 'class 55', the Deltic was built in 1961-62 by English Electric. It became one of the most powerful diesel-electric single-unit locomotives in the world, replacing the Mallard-type steam locomotives. It weighed a mighty 99 tonnes and had a maximum speed of 160km/h. With a brake force of 51 tonnes, the locomotive's speed record was 182km/h. In the 20 years that the Deltics worked the East Coast line between London and Edinburgh, they each ran more than five million kilometres.

MEGA FACT
In 1879, the first practical electric railway was demonstrated at an exhibition in Berlin. Designed and operated by German engineer Werner von Siemens, the locomotive, travelled at 6.5km/h and pulled 30 passengers.

RAILWAYS UNDERGROUND

The world's first underground railway was built in London, England, in 1863. A steam-powered railway was run just below the streets and connected the main line stations of Paddington to Farringdon Street. Until the installation of electric-powered trains in 1890, the 'tubes' – as they became known – were often smokey and hot. But they were quicker and more convenient than travelling by road. By the end of the 19th century other cities around the world began building their own underground railways.

MEGA FACT
One large passenger train can carry the same number of people as 100 cars.

Docklands Light Railway (DLR)

Light rail transit systems such as the DLR in London, England, provide an easy way to travel in a busy city. The DLR, installed in the Docklands in 1984-87, was designed to carry 2,000 passengers an hour in single cars. It became so popular that the system was rebuilt with multiple-unit trains to carry up to 12,000 passengers an hour. These 'driverless' trains are powered by electricity collected from a 'third rail' along the track, and are operated automatically by computer from a central control room.

CLASS 58

This powerful diesel-electric freight locomotive has a 3,300hp, 12-cylinder four-stroke turbo-charged V-engine. It is capable of hauling 1,000 tonnes on the level at 129km/h and was built to cope with the expected increase in coal traffic due to an oil crisis. The 'class 58' was built in Romania and delivered to British Railways in 1982. The main advantage of these locos was that the self-contained cabs could be disconnected, unbolted and replaced quickly. It often took months to repair a damaged cab on earlier British Rail diesels.

MEGA FACT
Electro-diesels require less servicing than diesel-electric trains, and have better acceleration. They also run more smoothly at high speed, which causes less wear.

RECORD BREAKERS

Since the first steam trains, railways have always tried to make and break speed records. For Britain and the USA, breaking the speed barrier of 160km/h was the first achievement. An American locomotive was claimed to have reached a speed of 181km/h in 1893, but this was never officially recognised. With new technology, attempts to beat new rail speed records will continue.

RACING ALONG THE RAILS

Owned and operated by SNCF, the French national railways, the TGV (Train à Grande Vitesse), is an electric train that runs between Paris and Lyon. For much of this route, the TGV runs on a special track at around 212km/h. Its top speed is 300km/h, although a modified TGV set a world record in 1990 when it reached 515.3km/h in trial runs. The TGV was developed as a high-speed system that was also compatible with the existing railway infrastructure where building new tracks or stations would have been too expensive.

Mail on the move

Until 1838, special mail coaches had delivered the Royal Mail. With the development of the railway passenger service in Britain, it was thought that a faster and more efficient service could be provided by rail. The travelling 'post office van' handled all the jobs that were carried out by a normal post office. It automatically picked up mail from specially designed lineside apparatus while still moving. After being sorted and put into sacks for different destinations along the route, the sacks were automatically dropped off into lineside nets. Railways are still used today by mail services, along with road and air transport.

EARLY SUCCESS

The TGV 001 prototype started an extensive testing programme in the early 1970s. It was powered by a gas turbine. On 8 December 1972, it set the world speed record for a train in autonomous traction, at 318km/h.

DOUBLE DECKER

The TGV Duplex was designed to maximise the number of people carried in one trainset. Its two seating levels can carry 545 passengers. The TGV Duplex is poised to become the busiest of the TGV fleet as orders for additional trainsets mount.

MEGA FACT

Most diesel engines power a generator, which makes electricity. This drives a motor that turns the wheels.

TGV (TRAIN À GRANDE VITESSE)

There is actually no such thing as the TGV and there are many big differences among the 350 or more trainsets in service today. The name 'TGV' refers to more than just the trains. It is a whole system, comprising of the train, the track and signalling technologies that, when combined, make high speeds possible. Almost all TGVs are made of steel. Weight saving features on the newest models, such as the TGV Duplex, include aluminium body shells and magnesium seat frames.

THE ICE

German InterCity Express (ICE) trains began public service in 1991, running daily from Hamburg to Munich via Frankfurt. The trains run mainly on upgraded existing lines, although special high-speed tracks are also used. During tests on these lines, the ICE set a German high-speed record of 404km/h, which held the world record for a short time.

X-2000 TILTING EXPRESS

Sweden's hilly countryside has made the building of new railway lines expensive, so they came up with the 'tilting' train. By 1990, the first twenty X-2000 tilting express trains, with a maximum speed of 210km/h were in operation. The tilting mechanism on these trains is controlled by an accelerometer at the front of the train. The degree of 'tilt' is limited to an amount where a passenger sitting on a corner seat on one side of a coach is no more than 300mm higher or lower than a passenger on the other side.

MEGA FACT
Most diesel engines power a generator, which makes electricity. This drives a motor that turns the wheels.

PACIFIC MALLARD

Designed by British engineer Sir Nigel Gresley, Mallard set a world speed record for a steam locomotive on 3 July 1938. Primarily on a special run to test braking, it achieved a speed of 203km/h on the descent of Stoke Bank between Grantham in Lincolnshire and Peterborough in Cambridgeshire, England. This record still stands, over 60 years later.

MEGA FACT
The Hiawatha Expresses were the fastest scheduled steam trains to ever run.

REACHING FOR THE SKY

Some rail systems run on or hang underneath rails attached to overhead structures. Overhead railways are relatively cheap to build and help to free ground space. There are two types. Suspended railways have trains hanging under the rail, with wheels that are fitted onto the rails. 'Straddle' railways are where a train fits over a single rail. Trains running on the 'straddle' system rest astride the rail and are guided by panels on either side of the rail. Overhead systems with a single rail are called 'monorails'.

NOT SO NEW

Overhead railways are not new. They are operated like any bus, heavy metro or conventional railway system. The Wuppertal, in Germany, was built in 1901. Wheel carriages hang from a single rail and are electrically driven. The system is so popular that it is suprising that more cities have not built this kind of monorail.

VERSATILE TRAVEL

Overhead rail systems are an efficient way to travel in congested cities, around theme parks – and skiers often use a monorail to travel from one mountain peak to another.

IS IT A PLANE?

In 1929, Scottish engineer George Bennie built a suspended monorail that travelled at 160km/h along a track using electric propellers. There were plans for a high-speed link between London and Paris, with a seaplane (Railplane) to carry passengers across the English Channel. Due to the world economic depression of the 1930s, the project did not progress past the experimental stage.

WUPPERTAL SCHWEBEBAHN

Designed by German engineer Eugen Langen, the Wuppertal Schwebebahn (swinging railway) has been in service since 1901. The entire system required over 19,000 tonnes of steel, with 472 steel supports carrying the track. By 1990, 16.7 million passengers a year were travelling on the Schwebebahn. The electric trains travel at 26.5km/h, although their top speed is 60km/h. For most of the 12.9km journey, the railway straddles the river Wupper.

MEGA FACT
The longest cableway in the world, between Boliden and Kristineberg in Sweden, was built in 1942 – and runs for 96km!

FUNICULAR RAILWAY

A funicular railway uses the technology of an elevator (a cable pulling a car up) and that of a railroad (a car on a track). A conventional train cannot travel up a steep incline because the steel train wheels do not have enough traction against steel rails. The funicular overcomes this by pulling the 'car' up by a cable. The wheels are only to guide the car. Funiculars use two cars at the same time, one on each side of the top pulley – one car balancing the weight of the other. The descending car's weight helps pull the ascending car up the mountain, and the ascending train keeps the speed of the descending train from going out of control. Funiculars have also been built for travel into caves and mines.

Elevated railway

Completed in 1870, New York's elevated railway was the first urban rapid transit system to be built in the USA. The need to move people between business districts and residential areas in Manhattan encouraged the development of alternative travel forms to road vehicles. Although the 'El' helped dissolve some of New York's street crowds, mechanical problems made the system unpopular for almost a decade. The steam locomotives pulling the wooden passenger cars were noisy and caused nearby buildings to shake. Walkers below the track also risked being hit by falling ash or oil.

MEGA FACT
The Qinghai-Tibet Railway in China is the highest — and longest in the world. When completed, the longest tunnel on the railway will be 1,720m long.

MONORAIL

Many of today's theme parks have their own specially built monorail systems. These monorails vary in size and style, but their basic purpose is to transport passengers. A large dual-rail system was built in Florida at Walt Disney World in 1975. The Tokyo/Haneda Monorail, built in Japan in 1964, was the first major system to use switches for direction reversal.

LATEST LOCOS

Today, fast, cheap flights and modern road transportation seem to be winning the war for carrying freight and passengers. Trains are often, though not always, seen as noisy, uncomfortable and crowded. But concerns about pollution and road congestion has lead to a renewed interest in trains. The latest trains are brighter, faster – and technologically sophisticated.

MAGNETIC PROPULSION

Maglev trains give passengers a very smooth, quiet ride. 'Maglev' is short for magnetic levitation. By using magnets to replace the traditional steel wheel and track trains, maglev trains are able to 'float' on a cushion of air above a metal track. This technique eliminates friction. The lack of friction and the trains' aerodynamics allows the vehicle to reach super speeds of 500km/h. Long-distance maglev services may well be the trains of the future, but today the tracks are still considered to be very expensive to build.

How a maglev train works

The maglev runs in a guideway. The train moves by magnets in the sides of the guideway and train. Magnets on the floor of the guideway repel the train's magnets, lifting it up 10cm. Magnets on the sides of the guideway and the train alternately attract and repel each other, pushing the train along.

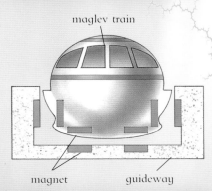

maglev train

magnet   guideway

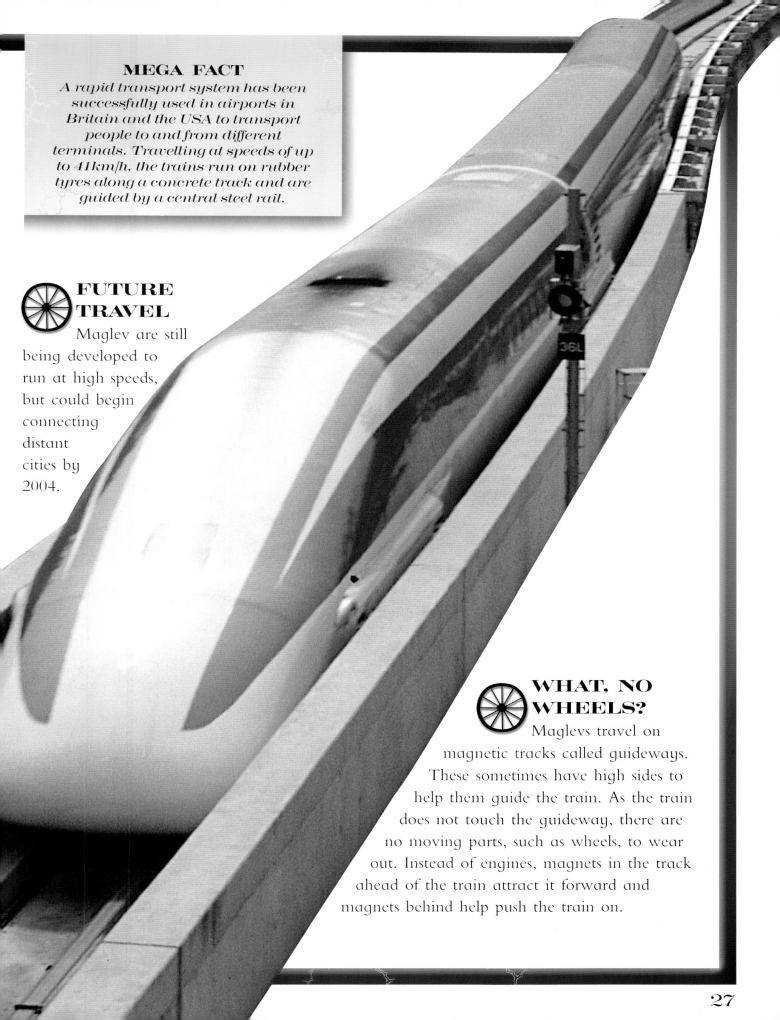

FUTURE TRAVEL

Maglev are still being developed to run at high speeds, but could begin connecting distant cities by 2004.

WHAT, NO WHEELS?

Maglevs travel on magnetic tracks called guideways. These sometimes have high sides to help them guide the train. As the train does not touch the guideway, there are no moving parts, such as wheels, to wear out. Instead of engines, magnets in the track ahead of the train attract it forward and magnets behind help push the train on.

EUROSTAR

Adopting the basic principles employed in the French TGV, designers made some important changes to the Eurostar. The main change was that it had to be able to operate in different countries. This meant that it had to be capable of using the electrical supply from three different systems, including current collection from a third rail in Britain. Operating from London between Paris and Brussels via the Channel Tunnel, Eurostar passenger trains have their own police and customs on board, as well as a prison compartment!

Maglev

Although they are based on similar concepts, the German and Japanese maglev trains have major differences. In Germany, engineers are building an electromagnetic suspension (EMS) system called 'Transrapid'. In this system, the bottom of the train wraps around a steel guideway (a magnetised coil running along a track). Electromagnets attached to the train's undercarriage are directed up toward the guideway. This levitates the train about 1cm above the guideway and keeps the train levitated even when it is not moving. The Japanese use an electrodynamic suspension (EDS) system for their version of the maglev (shown here), which is based on the repelling force of magnets.

SHINKANSEN

In the mid-1960s, Japan began a high-speed rail service between Tokyo and Osaka. The Shinkansen trains sped along at around 217km/h. Today, a 16-car Shinkansen, which is Japanese for 'new main line', can reach speeds of more than 268km/h. These locomotives became known as 'bullet' trains because of their sleek design. Apart from the original 3-abreast seats still fitted to some '0' and '200' series trains, all the seats in a Shinkansen car can be rotated either to face the direction of travel or to form bays of facing seats. The typical service life of a Shinkansen train is about 15 to 20 years.

VIRGIN'S PENDOLINO

A concept based on the way a motorcyclist combats centrifugal forces by leaning into a bend was behind the technology of the 'tilting' train. On 30 April 2002, London's Euston station was the venue for the first public showing of Virgin's Pendolino tilting train. Virgin Trains will eventually take delivery of 53 Pendolinos being built by Alstom in Birmingham, England. Already working successfully in Italy, Germany, Spain and Switzerland, each train has been designed to run at speeds of up to 225km/h. The train's tilt will enable it to negotiate bends at far greater speeds than conventional trains.

ARTICULATED LOCOMOTIVE   A locomotive that has two or more independent sets of frames joined together with independent groups of wheels, using pivots to increase flexibility.

BOGIE   A truck with a short wheelbase at the front of the locomotive, pivoted from the main frame.

CLASS   A category of locomotives built to a specific design.

COUPLED WHEELS   The driving wheels together with the wheels joined to them by the coupling-rod. This arrangement enables the power to be spread over several wheels, reducing wheel-slip.

CUT-OFF   The point in the piston stroke at which the admission of steam is stopped.

MEGA FACT

A diesel high-speed train with eight carriages and two locomotives is around 220m long.

9 Vrederust

HTM   HTM

3023

FLANGE A lip on the metal wheel of
a train, which keeps it on the tracks and
guides it around corners.

FRAME The structure of plates
or girders that supports the boiler
and wheels.

GAUGE The width between the two
rails on a railway track. In Britain,
North America and most of Europe, the
gauge is 1,435mm.

SLIDE VALVE A valve for controlling
steam admission and exhaust.

TANK LOCOMOTIVE A locomotive
that carries its fuel and water in bunkers
and tanks attached to the main frame, not
in a separate tender.

THIRD RAIL A length of rail built beside
the tracks that transmits electric power to
the engine.

TRACKING A term used to describe the
locomotive's ability to negotiate a curved
or irregular track.

TYPE A category of locomotive conforming
in function and basic layout, including wheel
arrangement.

WHEEL ARRANGEMENTS Steam
locomotives are often classified according
to the White system of notation. Wheel
arrangement can be front wheels,
driving wheels and rear
wheels. For example,
a '4-6-2' has four
front wheels, six
driving wheels and
two rear wheels. The
German system of
notation only counts
the wheels of one side,
so the above example
would be '2-3-1'.

INDEX

Locomotive Magazines:

✗ Heritage Railway
✗ British Railway
    Illustrated
✗ Locomotives
    Illustrated

✗ Steam Days
✗ The Arrow
✗ Railway World
✗ Traction

✗ Railways Digest
    Magazine
✗ Locomotive &
Railway Preservation
✗ Today's Railways

✗ Tramways & Urban
    Transit
✗ Speedlines
✗ Railway Age
✗ Modern Railways

Picture Credits

T=top; B=bottom; C=centre
Front cover Rail Images, 6-7 Milepost, 7 Milepost, 8T Mary Evans Picture Library, 8B
Milepost, 9T Underwood & Underwood/Corbis, 9B Mary Evans Picture Library, 10T
Milepost, 10B Colin Garratt, 11T&B Milepost, 12-13 Milepost, 14T Rail Images, 14B
Milepost, 15T&B Milepost, 16T&B Milepost, 17T Rail Images, 17B Milepost, 19T Milepost,
20T Rail Images, 20B Milepost, 21T Milepost, 21B Rail Images, 22-23 Milepost, 24T
Milepost, 24B Richard List/Corbis, 25T Mary Evans Picture Library, 26-27 Milepost, 28T
Rail Images, 28B Milepost, 29T&B Rail Images.
All other pictures Chrysalis Images.